NEIL DEGRASSE TYSON

NEIL DEGRASSE TYSON
STAR ASTROPHYSICIST

JILL SHERMAN

LERNER PUBLICATIONS ◆ MINNEAPOLIS

Lerner Publications Company
A division of Lerner Publishing Group, Inc.
241 First Avenue North
Minneapolis, MN USA 55401

For reading levels and more information, look up this title at www.lernerbooks.com.

Image credits: Desiree Navarro/WireImage/Getty Images, p. 2; Nicholas Hunt/Getty Images, p. 6; FOX Image Collection/Getty Images, pp. 8, 39; Mickey Adair/ Michael Ochs Archives/Getty Images, p. 9; TierneyMJ/Shutterstock.com, p. 11; Cem Ozdel/Anadolu Agency/Getty Images, pp. 12, 29; taffpixture/Shutterstock.com, p. 13; Jules Bucher/Science Source/Getty Images, p. 15; Spiroview Inc/Shutterstock.com, p. 17; Felix Mizioznikov/Shutterstock.com, p. 19; Debby Wong/ Shutterstock.com, p. 22; Todd Strand/Independent Picture Service, p. 23; alredosaz/Shutterstock.com, p. 24; Underwood Archives/Getty Images, p. 25; Sean Pavone/Shutterstock.com, p. 27; Scott Kowalchyk/CBS/Getty Images, p. 30; Andrew Toth/Getty Images, p. 32; Jason Kempin/ Getty Images, p. 36; Jim Spellman/WireImage/Getty Images, p. 37; Ben Molyneux/Alamy Stock Photo, p. 38; Taylor Hill/FilmMagic/Getty Images, p. 40.

Cover: Myrna Suarez/Contour/Getty Images.

Main body text set in Rotis Serif Std 55 Regular 13.5/17. Typeface provided by Adobe Systems.

Library of Congress Cataloging-in-Publication Data

Names: Sherman, Jill, author.
Title: Neil degrasse Tyson : star astrophysicist / Jill Sherman.
Description: Minneapolis : Lerner Publications, [2018] | Series: Gateway biographies | Audience: Ages 9–14. | Audience: Grades 4 to 6.
Identifiers: LCCN 2018010657 (print) | LCCN 2018004396 (ebook) | ISBN 9781541524491 (eb pdf) | ISBN 9781541524453 (lb : alk. paper)
Subjects: LCSH: Tyson, Neil deGrasse—Juvenile literature. | Astrophysicists—United States—Biography—Juvenile literature.
Classification: LCC QB460.72.T97 (print) | LCC QB460.72.T97 S54 2018 (ebook) | DDC 523.01092 [B]—dc23

LC record available at https://lccn.loc.gov/2018010657

Manufactured in the United States of America
1 - 44525 - 34775 - 4/16/2018

CONTENTS

Neil deGrasse Tyson speaks onstage at an event in 2016.

Now, come with me," Neil deGrasse Tyson said from a shiny metallic spacecraft as it took off toward the stars. The spacecraft was the Ship of the Imagination, and it could travel through time and space. From the ship, Tyson could explore the past, present, and future. He could explore the entirety of the cosmos. "To make this journey," he said, "we'll need imagination. But imagination alone is not enough because the reality of nature is far more wondrous than anything we can imagine."

As Tyson spoke, the Ship of the Imagination took off through space. It floated beyond Earth and approached the moon. It drifted past the blinding, burning sun. It dove through the clouds of Venus, soared over Mars, dodged asteroids and moons, and visited the storms of Jupiter. It continued on through the rings of Saturn before zooming past Uranus, Neptune, and the icy worlds beyond.

Then the ship left the solar system and went even farther. Tyson spoke of the stars and planets outside our solar system. He spoke of the Milky Way galaxy and its neighboring galaxies. Tyson spoke of the entire universe—a network of a hundred billion galaxies. And the universe may be bigger still than that. Other parts of the universe may be so far away that in the entire history of Earth, there has not been enough time for their light to reach us. "In the context of the cosmos," Tyson said, "we are small."

Tyson's journey took place on the first episode of his TV show, *Cosmos: A Spacetime Odyssey*, which aired

Tyson speaks about Earth in an episode of *Cosmos: A Spacetime Odyssey*.

on March 9, 2014. The show was a reboot of a show that had aired in 1980, called *Cosmos: A Personal Voyage.* The famous scientist Carl Sagan had hosted the original show, and it had been incredibly popular. More than five hundred million people in sixty countries watched. In the show, Sagan explained scientific topics. He spoke about the formation of the universe and the life cycle of stars. He described the history of astronomy and spoke of missions to send spacecraft to explore planets. He taught about comets, the possibility of life on Mars, and the development of life on Earth. Sagan spoke of the universe with a sense of wonder.

Tyson's show was similar. He spoke with the same sense of wonder for the universe, and he used several features that Sagan's show had, such as the computer-generated Ship of the Imagination. But Tyson also included updated visual effects and animations to show the big bang, explore the planets up close, and demonstrate what zero gravity might look like in

New York City. Tyson filmed parts of his show in Italy, France, and Iceland. He spoke of the vastness of the universe, and he explained how the galaxies and solar system had formed. He described the history of human understanding of space, and he talked about the origins of life on Earth. As Sagan did, Tyson thinks the universe is amazing. He also thinks that people need to understand science and know its importance in their everyday lives. "There's got to be at least one *Cosmos* a generation," he said. "Otherwise, we're not doing justice to sharing with the public the role of science and bringing the universe down to Earth."

Tyson has spent his whole life studying the universe, and he has dedicated his time to sharing his findings with others. He wants everyone to be as excited about the stars, the planets, and the mysteries of space as he is.

STAR CHILD

Neil was born on October 5, 1958. He has an older brother, Stephen, and younger sister, Lynn. His parents, Cyril and Sunchita Tyson, believed education was important. His father was a sociologist, someone who studies the development and structure of society. He worked to fight poverty and promote education in New York City. His mother became a gerontologist, someone who studies the science of aging, when Neil was in high school.

The Tysons encouraged their children to pursue their own interests. They taught them to express their ideas and to respect those who had different opinions. They knew that their children would face challenges due to racial prejudice. They believed that some teachers had lower expectations of African American students. So the Tysons made sure their children had opportunities to learn from experiences outside of school. Each weekend, the family visited museums and attended sports games, plays, or the opera.

Neil was a very social child, and he did not work hard to get good grades in school. His teachers often wished he would be more serious about his schoolwork. But despite his grades, Neil loved learning. He enjoyed thinking about brainteasers, especially ones that

Neil grew up in the Bronx, an area of New York City.

The Hayden Planetarium is part of the American Museum of Natural History in New York City.

involved math. And he became interested in science at a young age. At the age of nine, he knew he wanted to be an astrophysicist (someone who studies stars and other objects in space) when he grew up. He made this decision during his first visit to the Hayden Planetarium in New York City.

From his home in the Bronx, New York, Neil did not have the best view of the night sky. The tall buildings and city lights kept him from seeing many stars. The planetarium projected images of stars and constellations on its walls, so when Neil looked up there, he saw the night sky for the first time. It was beyond anything he had imagined. Stars were everywhere. He saw meteors flash across the sky. The instructor pointed out constellations on the northern horizon. He spotted a cloudy area—the Milky Way. Neil could hardly believe what he was seeing. He was hooked. From then on, Neil became obsessed with space.

From his apartment's rooftop, Neil could see only a handful of stars. A friend suggested he use binoculars to get a better look. Neil used them to look past the buildings and the streetlights. Then he got his first good look at the moon.

With the binoculars, Neil was able to see more than simply the pale, round light he had always known. He

Sometimes the moon looks like a plain round object in the night sky. With binoculars or a telescope, much more detail becomes visible.

saw the moon's surface in detail. He could see its valleys, craters, and hills. Suddenly, the moon seemed like a real place. And it made Neil think about all the other places beyond the moon. They were just as real and held even more mystery.

When Neil was in seventh grade, he upgraded his binoculars to a telescope. Neil studied the sky constantly. He especially liked looking at Saturn. It didn't matter if it was cold outside or if snow was on the ground. As long as he had a clear view of the sky, Neil was outside with his telescope.

It wasn't long, however, before Neil had outgrown the limits of his first telescope. He began saving his money to buy a bigger, better telescope. To earn extra money, he started walking dogs. He charged fifty cents per walk. With his savings and some help from his parents, Neil bought a new telescope.

He took the large telescope up to the rooftop every night to look at the sky. Neighbors seeing him from their windows sometimes thought he was a prowler. Several people reported Neil to the police for his suspicious behavior. When the police arrived, Neil happily offered them a look at the stars and planets above.

STUDYING THE SKY

Along with studying the sky on his own, Neil began taking astronomy classes from experts at the Hayden

Planetarium. In his favorite class, he learned about the big bang and black holes.

In June 1973, Neil received a scholarship to take the SS *Canberra* to Mauritania, in northwestern Africa, along with two thousand scientists, engineers, and astronomers. There, on June 30, they would be able to view a total solar eclipse, which occurs when the moon moves in front of the sun, completely blocking the sun's light. This eclipse lasted for seven minutes—it was one of the longest solar eclipses ever recorded.

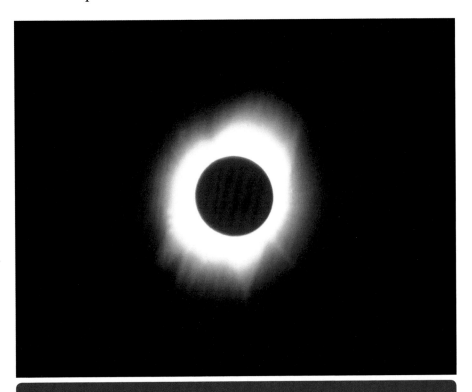

This image of the 1973 solar eclipse was taken from Kenya, in East Africa.

Later that summer, Neil went on another astronomy trip—this time to the southwestern United States. He hopped in a van with other teenage astronomers, and they drove fifty-three hours to arrive at Camp Uraniborg in the Mojave Desert of Southern California.

Here, far from any city lights, billions of stars lit up the sky. Neil was stunned. He hadn't seen anything like it outside of the Hayden Planetarium. For a month, Neil stayed up until all hours of the night using the camp's high-performance telescopes to look at the stars. He also took courses in math and astrophysics, and he learned how to program a computer.

Neil returned home full of excitement about the things he had seen and learned. He brought back a series of photographs he had taken of planets and stars. A family friend was a professor at City College of New York. She recommended Neil to another professor at the college, who invited Neil to speak in one of her classes. He showed his photographs and spoke enthusiastically about stars and comets to a room of fifty adult students. "It was as natural as breathing," he later said about the experience. "I was just talking about what I knew, the way other boys talked about baseball cards."

What's more, he was paid fifty dollars for his service. For Neil, this was a small fortune. In an hour of talking about his favorite subject, he'd earned what would have taken him one hundred dog walks.

In 1976 Neil was a senior at the Bronx High School of Science. He was captain of the wrestling team and

City College of New York

editor in chief of the school's physical science journal. As graduation approached, he had to decide which college to attend. His top picks were MIT, Harvard, and Cornell. The Cornell Admissions Department noticed Neil's interest in physics and shared a copy of his application with one of their professors, Carl Sagan. Soon after, Neil received a personal letter from Sagan. Sagan wanted to meet him.

On a snowy Saturday in December, Neil rode a bus to Ithaca, New York, to visit Cornell University. Sagan gave Neil a tour of his lab and a signed copy of one of his books. And at the end of the visit, Sagan drove Neil to the bus station. It was snowing, and Sagan wrote down his home phone number for Neil. He told Neil to call if the bus couldn't get back because of the snow. If Neil couldn't make it home, he could spend the night at Sagan's home.

This meeting with Sagan had a profound influence on Neil. He already knew he wanted to be a scientist. But talking with Sagan showed him what kind of person he wanted to be. At the time, it wasn't very common for African Americans to pursue careers in science. "I was doing something people of my skin color were not supposed to do," Tyson later said. "So people who believed in me, like Sagan, were important." For the rest of his life, Neil would make sure to treat others with the same kindness and respect that Sagan had shown him.

Despite Neil's experience with Sagan, Neil wasn't convinced to choose Cornell. Instead, he made a spreadsheet using the articles he read in the science magazine *Scientific American*. He read the About the Authors section in each magazine and wrote down which schools the magazine's writers had attended or where they were professors. Harvard showed up most often in the spreadsheet. So Neil was off to Harvard.

TEACHING AND TRAINING

In 1976 Tyson began studying physics (a science that has to do with matter and energy) at Harvard University. He

Harvard University in Cambridge, Massachusetts, is one of the world's most well-known and respected universities.

received some scholarships to attend the school, but he also earned money by cleaning student bathrooms in the dorms. He later said it was one of the strangest jobs he ever had. He earned his bachelor's degree in 1980, and then he went to the University of Texas in Austin, where he began working to earn a PhD. He wrote a column for the school's astronomy magazine *StarDate*. Every month, under the name Merlin, Tyson answered questions from readers. It was a great way for Tyson to share his knowledge of astronomy with the public. His answers were short and direct to help people understand topics such as Earth's rotation and the size of the Milky Way galaxy.

Tyson also worked as a teaching assistant and a math tutor while he was at the University of Texas. His professors said he had a natural gift for teaching–Tyson's students loved having him in class. Tyson experimented with interesting ways to communicate with his students. He sometimes even danced in front of the class. Once he copied Michael Jackson's famous moonwalk dance for his students.

"If you're only using words to communicate as a teacher, why show up?" Tyson says. "Why not just type your notes? Teaching is a full-body performance. The moonwalk was all the rage in 1983, and the students loved it. It made the material work for them."

However, Tyson's time in Texas was a struggle in some ways. Most PhD students spend their time researching and studying a specific topic to write a paper called a dissertation. But Tyson had other interests besides his research. He was on the wrestling team, and he participated in competitive rowing and ballroom dance. Tyson knew he should spend more time in the physics lab. He was serious about his studies, but he also thought it was important to participate in other activities. Tyson's professors did not think he was making enough progress in his research, and they encouraged him to pursue a different career.

Along with his academic struggles, Tyson faced racism at the University of Texas. At the time, very few African

PASSION FOR DANCE

Tyson began to take an interest in dance while he was at Harvard University. He learned a number of styles, including ballet, jazz, Afro-Caribbean, and Latin ballroom. He continued dancing at the University of Texas. In 1985 Tyson won a gold medal at a national tournament in Latin ballroom dance with the university dance team. Tyson had been a wrestler for many years, so he was strong and flexible. He thought dance was interesting because it took those qualities a step further. As he put it, "[Dance asks] Can you be graceful? Can you move your body in a way where you are fully aware of what every muscle is doing?" He explained that "I just valued that, almost with an academic curiosity."

American students were studying physics there. People thought Tyson must be an athlete. They didn't believe that he could be a physics student. "I was stopped and questioned seven times by University police on my way into the physics building," Tyson said. "Seven times. Zero times was I stopped going into the gym—and I went to the gym a lot. That says all you need to know about how welcome I felt at Texas." Tyson earned his master's degree from the university in 1983, but he did not continue with his PhD. His professors decided he had failed in his studies.

COMING HOME

Tyson returned to New York in 1988. That year he also married Alice Young, who he had met in a class in Texas. She too had studied math and physics, and she earned her PhD from the University of Texas in 1985. Back home in New York and starting a new life with his wife, Tyson decided to continue his academic career at Columbia University. He studied the chemicals that make up stars in the galactic bulge, the area in the center of most spiral galaxies (galaxies in which the stars gather in spiral arms that spread out from the center). Tyson earned a master of philosophy degree in astrophysics in 1989.

Tyson and his wife, Alice Young, attend an event together in 2014.

Merlin's Tour of the Universe uses scientific information, humor, and stories about historical figures such as Leonardo da Vinci and Albert Einstein to answer questions about the universe.

MERLIN'S TOUR OF THE UNIVERSE

NEIL DE GRASSE TYSON

While he was at Columbia, Tyson put his old columns from *StarDate* together into a book called *Merlin's Tour of the Universe*. The book, published in 1989, answered common questions about astronomy. Tyson also had his first TV interview. The reporter asked him about solar flares, or sudden explosions of light and energy on the sun. When Tyson watched the interview later, he realized it was the first time he had ever seen an African American interviewed on TV as an expert about something other than sports, entertainment, or race. Tyson realized that his science career could have value in society beyond simply educating people about science. He

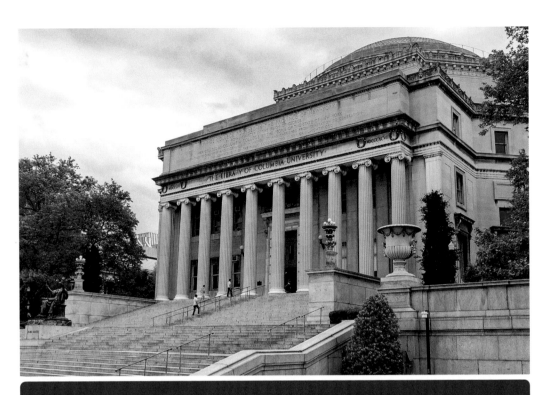

Columbia University

also had a voice as one of only a few African Americans with an advanced degree in astrophysics. When Tyson earned his PhD from Columbia in 1991, he was just the seventh African American astrophysicist in the United States.

By 1994 Tyson had published a second book. *Universe Down to Earth*, a collection of essays, explained the life cycle of stars, elements on the periodic table, the big bang, and black holes. Tyson didn't use difficult scientific language to explain these topics. Instead, he wrote in a way that even those without a scientific background could understand.

Around this time, the Hayden Planetarium was looking for a new director. A professor of astrophysics at Princeton University recommended Tyson for the position, and in 1996, Tyson began working at the very place that had inspired him to become an astrophysicist. One of the first projects Tyson took on in his new job was updating the planetarium. The planetarium had first opened in 1935. Then constellations were a major part of astronomy. However, by the 1990s, telescopes had become more advanced, and scientists were studying

Workers finish the entryway to the Hayden Planetarium in 1935.

other things in space such as black holes. Tyson wanted the planetarium to reflect these changes. He also wanted to create more opportunities to educate the public about astronomy.

In 1997 the old Hayden Planetarium was demolished. Three years later, the rebuilding project was finished. The new planetarium included updated projectors to display an accurate depiction of the night sky. New videos taught about the formation of the moon and whether life might exist on other planets.

Like the original, the updated planetarium hosted educational programs. Astronomers gave presentations on radio telescopes, exoplanets, and the formation of the solar system. Tyson also created a new department focused on research. He hired fifteen astrophysicists who would focus on studying the universe, making discoveries, and keeping the planetarium up to date on the latest scientific information. Tyson hoped that the new planetarium would inspire a new generation of scientists, just as it had inspired him.

STAR POWER

When the Hayden Planetarium reopened in 2000, it had about one thousand visitors each hour for the first year. People were excited about the updated exhibits, but Tyson also faced some criticism. One exhibit classified the planets, asteroids, and other objects in the solar

Hayden Planetarium, 2012

system. At the time, most people considered Pluto to be the ninth planet in the solar system. However, Pluto was not labeled as a planet in the planetarium's exhibit. Instead, the exhibit display said, "Beyond the outer planets is the Kuiper Belt of comets, a disk of small, icy worlds including Pluto." Most visitors did not notice that the exhibit did not call Pluto a planet, but those who did thought it must have been a mistake. Tyson received angry letters criticizing the exhibit. It wasn't until years later that people began to recognize that Tyson's exhibit was accurate.

RECLASSIFYING PLUTO

In 1992 astronomers spotted rocky, icy objects orbiting beyond Pluto, in an area known as the Kuiper Belt. Soon astronomers knew of about seventy of these objects in the Kuiper Belt. The objects were similar to Pluto. Scientists were beginning to think Pluto might simply be the largest of these objects rather than a planet. Tyson agreed with this idea. That's why he did not label Pluto a planet in the Hayden Planetarium.

In 2006 the International Astronomical Union (IAU), an organization for professional astronomers, officially decided that Pluto was not a planet. The union created a new definition of a planet. For scientists to consider an object in space a planet, it must orbit the sun and be round, and the area around the object's orbit must be clear of other objects. Pluto did not meet this last requirement. The area around Pluto was filled with other icy Kuiper Belt objects. So the International Astronomical Union officially reclassified Pluto as a dwarf planet. Dwarf planets are similar to planets, but they do not have orbits clear of other objects. Other dwarf planets in the Kuiper Belt include Ceres, Eris, and Makemake. Astronomers think that more than one hundred dwarf planets may be in the solar system.

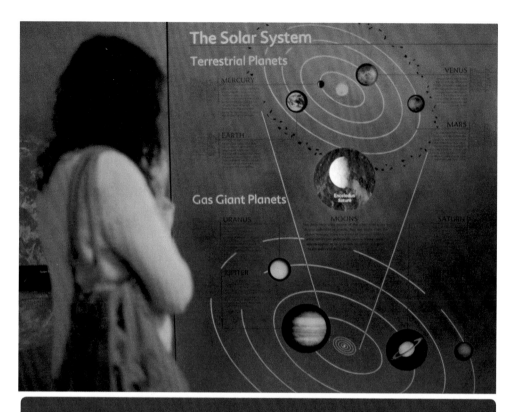

This diagram is part of the solar system exhibit at the Hayden Planetarium.

While working at the Hayden Planetarium, Tyson continued to write books and magazine articles about astronomy. In 2000 he released the book *One Universe: At Home in the Cosmos.* Tyson also edited a book of science essays called *Cosmic Horizons: Astronomy at the Cutting Edge,* and he wrote a column called Universe for *Natural History* magazine. By 2001 Tyson was well known as someone who could explain science to the public in an interesting and easy-to-understand way. President George W. Bush appointed Tyson to two government committees to discuss space exploration and research. Tyson also appeared on many television programs to discuss the latest scientific discoveries. Many major news networks are near the Hayden Planetarium, so when producers were looking for a scientist to talk on camera about meteor showers or passing comets, they could count on Tyson for an interview.

Tyson was a frequent guest on talk shows too. Shows such as *The Daily Show with Jon Stewart*, *The Colbert Report*, and *Late Night with Conan O'Brien* invited Tyson to talk about his books, discuss science fiction films, and share interesting information about space. Stephen

Tyson speaks with Stephen Colbert on *The Late Show with Stephen Colbert* in 2018.

Colbert, the host of *The Colbert Report*, said Tyson was one of his favorite people to have on the show because Tyson could answer questions that everyone wonders about, such as "Why is the sky blue?" Tyson was on Colbert's show eight times.

In 2004 Tyson had another opportunity to appear on television. But this time, he wouldn't be giving an interview. Instead, Tyson hosted a four-part miniseries called *Origins*. On the show, Tyson explained how the universe began, how Earth formed, and how life on Earth evolved. He wanted to help people understand the history of the universe and make it relevant to their everyday lives. Tyson focused on up-to-date research and spoke with people who were working in the field of astronomy. This made the series interesting for both scientists and those without a science background.

A POP SCIENCE ICON

Following the success of *Origins*, Tyson looked for new ways to share his love of science with the public. In 2009 Tyson began hosting a radio show called *StarTalk* with comedian Lynne Koplitz. On the show, they discussed space, science, and popular culture.

Tyson later took over as host and brought in a different comedian each week. Guest hosts included talk show host John Oliver and comedians such as Eugene Mirman and Kristen Schaal. On *StarTalk*, Tyson can

Tyson participates in a discussion about climate change in 2014.

focus on the science topic, and he knows the comedian will help make the show more entertaining. The successful radio show and podcast has launched spinoff shows including *StarTalk All-Stars*, hosted by various scientists, and *StarTalk Playing with Science*, which combines science and sports. A *StarTalk* television series airs on the National Geographic Channel.

Many scientists share their studies with other scientists through academic conferences and articles in science journals. But they are not always very good at sharing their ideas with the public. Tyson knows that many people spend hours each day watching television or looking at social media, so he thinks it's important to present science not just in academic settings but also in pop culture. Tyson has appeared on the TV show *The Big Bang Theory*, and he has been depicted in *The Simpsons* and an issue of *Action Comics* in which he helps Superman find his home planet, Krypton.

Tyson has a huge online following too. He has more than twelve million followers on Twitter, and he posts about science, current events, and even football. In one popular tweet, he said that Earth's rotation likely influenced the motion of a Cincinnati Bengals field goal.

Tyson is also a popular interviewee for the website Reddit's Ask Me Anythings (AMAs). In AMAs Reddit users can ask an interviewee questions on any topic. Tyson has answered a wide variety of questions about science and celebrities he has met. He is responsible for some of the most popular AMAs of all time.

One of the things Tyson is most famous for is his movie critiques. When movies about science or space come out, Tyson points out any bad science he sees in them. Tyson has dissected movies such as *Gravity* (2013), *Interstellar* (2014), *The Martian* (2015), and *Guardians of the Galaxy 2* (2017).

In *Guardians of the Galaxy 2*, for example, Tyson takes issue with the battle scenes. In these scenes, as characters shoot down other spacecraft, explosions boom all around. But Tyson points out that space is silent. If the filmmakers wanted to show these scenes accurately, there would be no sound at all.

ENTHUSIASTIC EDUCATION

In 2009 Tyson met with actor, producer, and comedian Seth MacFarlane. MacFarlane was concerned that students in the United States often perform poorly on international science and math exams and that the general public does not have a very good understanding of many scientific topics. MacFarlane wanted to create a television show based on science. He believed that Tyson was just the person to help him.

Working with producers and writers, MacFarlane and Tyson created *Cosmos: A Spacetime Odyssey*. The hit show's thirteen episodes explored the mysteries of the universe, from the formation of the solar system to the origins of life and human understanding and exploration

THE GOD QUESTION

People often ask scientists about religion and God. Many people think that religion is at odds with scientific discoveries. For example, many Christians believe that God created the universe, Earth, and life on Earth. However, scientists say that the big bang formed the universe, gravity and physics formed Earth, and life on Earth evolved over millions of years. Christians and scientists often debate their different ideas about the origins of the universe. When Tyson is asked whether there is a God, he says he doesn't know. In a video that has been viewed more than two million times, Tyson says that many people think he is an atheist—someone who does not believe in God. Tyson prefers to say he is agnostic—he believes that God's existence is unknowable.

Tyson says that science is a way of thinking and that through scientific thinking people come to understand what is true about the universe. Tyson thinks that it is important to have evidence to know whether something is true. He says, "I cannot look at the universe and say that 'yes there's a god and this god cares about my life at all.' The evidence does not support this." Ultimately, Tyson prefers to identify simply as a scientist. He says it is more important to be curious about the world than to debate whether God exists.

Tyson and Seth MacFarlane attend the premiere of *Cosmos: A Spacetime Odyssey* in 2014.

of space. About 8.5 million viewers tuned in for the first episode.

Meanwhile, Tyson was writing and publishing new books. *The Pluto Files: The Rise and Fall of America's Favorite Planet* was released in 2009. *Space Chronicles: Facing the Ultimate Frontier* came out in 2012, and *Welcome to the Universe: An Astrophysical Tour* was published in 2016.

BEST FRIENDS WITH BILL NYE

Tyson often makes public appearances with fellow science educator Bill Nye, host of the popular PBS show *Bill Nye the Science Guy* and the 2017 Netflix show *Bill Nye Saves the World*. Nye and Tyson have become good friends. They text and email each other several times a week. They've even spent Thanksgiving together.

Nye and Tyson are both dedicated to educating the public about science. They speak out when people question science. For example, some people do not believe that climate change, or changes to weather patterns on Earth, is really occurring. However, most scientists agree that human activity is contributing to climate change, which leads to melting glaciers and rising sea levels. Bill Nye has appeared on CNN and Fox to explain the science of climate change.

Tyson and Bill Nye appear at an event in New York City in 2017.

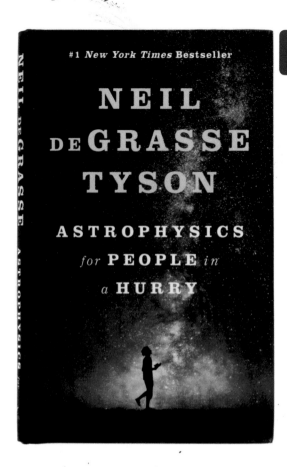

Tyson's most recent book, *Astrophysics for People in a Hurry,* came out in 2017. It quickly became a best seller. The book's chapters are short and easy to read, so readers don't have to spend a lot of time trying to understand difficult scientific language. Tyson knows that people often hear about things such as exoplanets, dark matter, and the multiverse but don't necessarily understand what they are. He wanted to make sure that nonscientists could understand these complicated parts of the universe that astrophysicists study.

Tyson wants to make astrophysics fun and exciting. His enthusiasm for science and space exploration draws people in. But Tyson also makes sure to present topics that he knows he can explain well. He chooses fascinating topics and the most amazing information. He is careful not to oversimplify science. Instead, he describes it using popular culture or other references that will make the science more relevant and easy to understand.

In 2018 Tyson was thrilled to find out that Fox had renewed *Cosmos* for another season. Tyson and MacFarlane both agreed to work on the new series. *Cosmos: Possible Worlds* aims to take a hopeful view of the future. New ideas in science can improve our

Tyson poses for a photo to promote *Cosmos*.

Tyson speaks at an event about the future of technology in 2015.

way of life. Tyson believes that when people embrace scientific discoveries and devote time and money to research, society will be safer, healthier, and wealthier. By teaching people about science, Tyson is doing his part to ensure there is a bright future ahead.

Throughout all his other work, Tyson has continued to serve as the director of the Hayden Planetarium. He still devotes much of his time to education and public appearances. Tyson receives hundreds of requests to give presentations each month. Because he is so busy, he can't accept all of these invitations, but he loves having the opportunity to talk to the public about science. Following his talks, audience members often crowd around to ask him more questions. He gladly participates in these conversations, not only because science is his favorite subject but also because he wants to help people understand the world and to think about new ideas. Tyson believes we need creative ways to interest people in science. And if Tyson's past is any indication, he has no shortage of ideas.

IMPORTANT DATES

1958   Neil deGrasse Tyson is born on October 5 in New York.

1966   He visits the Hayden Planetarium for the first time.

1976   He graduates from the Bronx High School of Science.

1980   He graduates from Harvard University with a degree in physics.

1983   Tyson completes a master's degree in astronomy at the University of Texas.

1985   He publishes his first research paper in the *Astrophysics Journal*.

1988   He marries Alice Young.

1989   He publishes his first book, *Merlin's Tour of the Universe*.

1991   He earns a PhD in astrophysics from Columbia University.

1996	He joins the staff at the Hayden Planetarium.
2001	President George W. Bush appoints Tyson to serve on a commission advising on aerospace.
2004	Tyson hosts *Origins*.
2007	He publishes *Death by Black Hole*.
2009	He begins hosting the weekly podcast *StarTalk*.
2014	He hosts the television series *Cosmos: A Spacetime Odyssey*.
2015	He hosts the *StarTalk* television series.
2017	He publishes *Astrophysics for People in a Hurry*.

SOURCE NOTES

7 Neil deGrasse Tyson, "Standing Up in the Milky Way," *Cosmos: A Spacetime Odyssey*, episode 1, aired March 9, 2014, on Fox.

8 Tyson.

10 Megan Gannon, "Inside 'Cosmos': Q&A with Host Neil deGrasse Tyson," *Space.com*, March 7, 2014, https://www.space.com /24952-cosmos-tv-series-neil-degrasse-tyson-interview.html.

16 Rose Cahalan, "Star Power," *Alcalde*, February 28, 2012, http:// alcalde.texasexes.org/2012/02/star-power/.

18 Cahalan.

20 Cahalan.

21 Cahalan.

21 Larry Getlen, "Dancing with the Stars: Neil deGrasse Tyson Talks Ballroom, Comedy and Football," *Observer*, October 22, 2015, http://observer.com/2015/10/dancing-with-the-stars-neil -degrasse-tyson-talks-ballroom-comedy-and-pretty-sunsets/.

27 Kenneth Chang, "Pluto's Not a Planet? Only in New York," *New York Times*, January 22, 2001, http://www.nytimes.com/2001 /01/22/nyregion/pluto-s-not-a-planet-only-in-new-york.html.

35 Kelly Dickerson, "Neil deGrasse Tyson Has a Hilarious Reason for Not Believing in Intelligent Design," *Business Insider*, November 8, 2015, http://www.businessinsider.com/neil-degrasse-tyson-god -religion-2015-11.

SELECTED BIBLIOGRAPHY

Cahalan, Rose. "Star Power." *Alcalde*, February 28, 2012. http://alcalde
.texasexes.org/2012/02/star-power/.

Druyan, Ann, and Steven Soter. *Cosmos: A Spacetime Odyssey*. Directed
by Brannon Braga. Los Angeles: 21st Century Fox, 2014.

Getlen, Larry. "Dancing with the Stars: Neil deGrasse Tyson Talks
Ballroom, Comedy and Football." *Observer*, October 22, 2015. http://
observer.com/2015/10/dancing-with-the-stars-neil-degrasse-tyson-talks
-ballroom-comedy-and-pretty-sunsets/.

Heller, Karen. "Star Talker: Neil deGrasse Tyson on Fame, Education,
and Tweets." *Washington Post*, February 24, 2015. https://www
.washingtonpost.com/lifestyle/style/star-talker-neil-degrasse-tyson
-on-fame-education-and-tweets/2015/02/24/5ec101fa-b854-11e4-a200
-c008a01a6692_story.html?noredirect=on&utm_term=.5dac725924b8

Mead, Rebecca. "Starman." *New Yorker*, February 17, 2014. https://www
.newyorker.com/magazine/2014/02/17/starman.

Tyson, Neil de Grasse. *Astrophysics for People in a Hurry*. New York:
W. W. Norton, 2017.

——. *The Sky Is Not the Limit*. New York: Doubleday, 1994.

FURTHER READING

BOOKS

Culp, Jennifer. *Neil deGrasse Tyson*. New York: Rosen, 2015. Read more about Tyson's journey from a kid who loved looking at the sky to one of the world's most recognizable scientists.

Roland, James. *Pluto: A Space Discovery Guide*. Minneapolis: Lerner Publications, 2017. Read more about Pluto, how it was discovered, and how we continue to explore this distant dwarf planet.

Saucier, C. A. P. *Explore the Cosmos like Neil deGrasse Tyson: A Space Science Journey*. Amherst, NY: Prometheus Books, 2015. Learn more about Tyson, and explore up-to-date information about astrophysics and the science of the universe.

Space! New York: DK, 2015. Discover more about the wonders of the universe that excite Tyson, including the big bang, black holes, and space travel.

Tyson, Neil deGrasse. *StarTalk*. Young Readers ed. Washington, DC: National Geographic. 2018. Find out the answers to all your questions about the world, with Tyson's funny book that discusses everything from climate change and Mars to superheroes and the human brain.

WEBSITES

National Geographic
http://channel.nationalgeographic.com/cosmos-a-spacetime
-odyssey/
Find articles and videos about Tyson and his show *Cosmos: A Spacetime Odyssey.*

Neil deGrasse Tyson
http://www.haydenplanetarium.org/tyson/
Learn more about the world's most popular astrophysicist, his books, and the Hayden Planetarium.

StarTalk
https://www.startalkradio.net/
Access episodes of *StarTalk*, and learn about the science involved in music, sports, and technology.

INDEX